# Knock on My Door

## Sarah Morris

*Smith/Doorstop Books*

Published 2008 by
Smith/Doorstop Books
The Poetry Business
The Studio
Byram Arcade
Westgate
Huddersfield HD1 1ND

Copyright © Sarah Morris 2008
All Rights Reserved

ISBN 978-1-902382-97-5
Designed and typeset at The Poetry Business
Printed by Swiftprint, Huddersfield

Cover design and illustrations by Sarah Morris
Author's photograph: Kimberley Tilger-Holt

The Poetry Business gratefully acknowledges the help of Arts Council England and Kirklees Culture and Leisure Services.

## *Introduction*

My name is Sarah Morris. I have Downs Syndrome. I am special. I am 35 years old. I am very close to all my family. I do creative things: art, poetry, swimming and dancing, taking photos and filming all over the countryside. I am an actress on television on Inside Out and Emmerdale. I work at the theatre with 'Full Body and the Voice'.

I wrote this book about my life and friends and family. I have enjoyed writing poems about them in my world.

These poems come out of my head in words, and Helen helps me with ideas. This book belongs to me in my special heart to share the skills I learnt with others.

I hope this book inspires other people to be creative with art and poems.

## *Thanks*

I want to thank these people:

Kim my personal assistant for supporting me with my work

AIM (Artists in Mind) for the use of the art studio to do my art and poems in

Helen for her friendship with me

Janet for publishing my poems

My special family, my mum and dad for supporting me in my flat and loving me in my relaxing heart

Scope, Kirklees Council and Karlie from United Response, for helping me with my Direct Payments

the rest of my family and friends:
    Rebecca and Richard and Frankie
    Francis and Peter
    Hilary and David
    cousins in Australia and Norway
    Brenda and Jack and Helen
    Janice and Eileen

## *Contents*

| | |
|---|---|
| 3 | Introduction |
| 5 | Thanks |
| 6 | Contents |
| 7 | When I was a child |
| 8 | My sister |
| 9 | My Gran |
| 10 | Helen |
| 11 | My family in my life |
| 12 | Full Body and the Voice Actors |
| 13 | Butterfly World |
| 14 | Dream Cave |
| 15 | Star |
| 16 | Lakes |
| 17 | Power |
| 18 | Flying |
| 19 | My Open Book |
| 20 | Journey |
| 21 | Over the Rainbow |
| 22 | Scene Changes |
| 23 | Shine on My Path |
| 24 | My Light |
| 25 | Special Heart |
| 26 | Knock on My Door |
| 27 | I Remember ... |

## *When I was a child*

I was born at home.
My mum and dad love me.
I was Downs Syndrome
      my mum was upset
           I nearly died
but I survived

## *My sister*

When I was a child
walk down on my memory of a journey
    to see my sister
    in the
    golden mirror
    to see
my sister when she was born
    in hospital
    in a cot.

## *My Gran*

A candle light shine
      over
      the night
to see my shadow in the
    sea of light
walk down on my path
    to see a bird
    fly in the sky
carrying my heart
      to my Gran

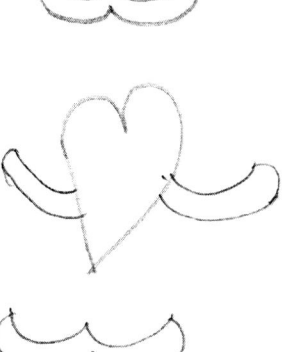

## *Helen*

My heart dripping down
     into
  Helens heart
walk down on Helens path
  candle light shine
  into Helens life
  Over the rainbow
     faraway
  across the sky
Shining colours through my
    life
  in a dark night
  Twinkle little star
    shine
  in Helens heart

## *My family in my life*

Open my book
to see
my family
all around my heart
love me
all around
in
golden water
to see them
echos around the cave
a light shine in a big wave
my life is in my future
with my family.

## *Full Body and the Voice Actors*

My dream will be an actress on
the stage
a big cheer to clap
light up my world of friends
in a hot air balloon
a Queen Victoria
waving
her flag
in the sunlight
music of the night
in candle light

# *Butterfly World*

Flying colours on the earth
moving around in the space
    over the rainbow
      on top of my world
    flapping my wings
    in the wind
inside a warm
    tropical world
        on the earth

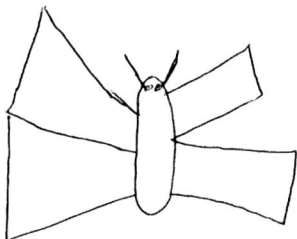

## *Dream Cave*

Open my heart in the door
step inside my
dark cave
close my eyes
follow my light
going down
falling down into the
land of colours
on the journey through
the cave
of light

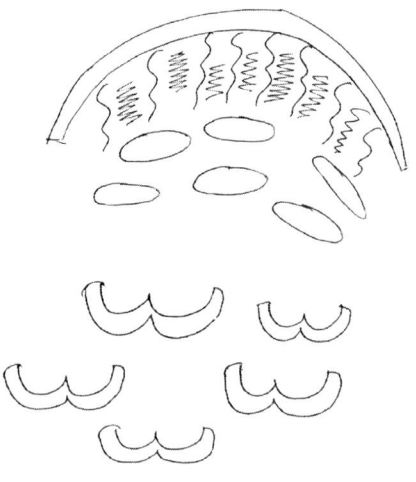

## *Star*

Falling star coming down
      through the Heaven
        fall down
        into the earth
     magic dust in the sunset
  in the night
sailing on the sea
  in my dreams

## *Lakes*

Looking glass lake
    reflecting
    lilac mountains
    yellow flowers
        open out
        in summer
a sun beaming down
    through the
    trees
Cracking branches on
    the ground

## *Power*

Lightning across the
> Rainbow

Heart beat in the world
> of freedom

Sun beaming down
> into darkness
>> of light

on the earth

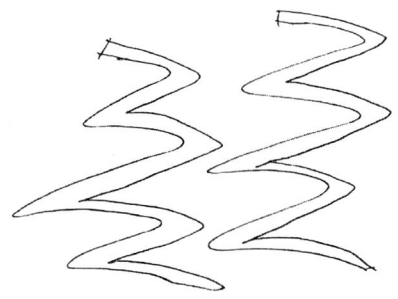

## *Flying*

Over over to my world
    of heart
        burning inside my feelings
  a boat sailing across
    Atlantic Ocean
on a journey across the sea
      around the circles
to another side of Australia
    banging like fireworks
      in the night

## *My Open Book*

Open my door to see
      my world of sun and light
          walk down on my path
            through
            the
            door
      walk down on my golden ribbon
        around my heart
to hear the birds
singing in the sunlight
      open my gate to see Kims life
          to look back with her brothers
            in the mirror

## *Journey*

On a journey through the snow
        a train going by
flying ticket in a dark
        sky
a light shine in my dream
    close my eyes
into the moonlight
        in my world
Dancing puppets in the night
Christmas lights flashing colours
        in a dark cave
    moving stars chasing
        up and down
        slide goes down down down
      into my world of light

## *Over the Rainbow*

No place like home
Somewhere over the rainbow
  follow yellow brick road
    into my heart
go on my journey through
    the forest
      in the dark
        to see Lion
          on my journey follow my path
           a bed of flowers
            in my dream
            knock on my dream
              door
          Hold my hands
            on crystal ball
            click my magic
              slippers
            close my eyes
            no place like
              home

## *Scene Changes*

Wet clothes on a journey
across the sea
hang out with pegs drip drip drip
sun comes out in the sky
dry dry
the wind blows the clothes
swaying swaying
walk down on my path
to see
a world of life
to see
clothes on the line
a basket fly fly
across the sky
to another world
a place of paradise

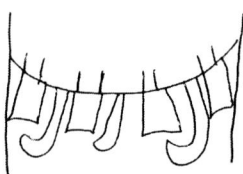

## *Shine on My Path*

Sunset shine through the sky
       On my path
Go down to see my friends in the light
       On my path
Around my heart in the world
Shining colours like a rainbow
Stars twinkle in the night
          On my path
Shooting star through the forest
Sailing along in sea light

On my path.

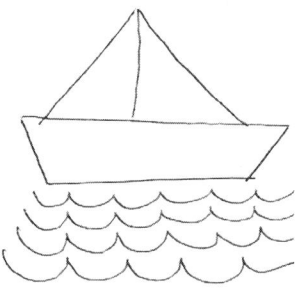

## My Light

In a dark dark sky
clouds going by
light shine
through like a moon
shine on me
when I was a child

## *Special Heart*

Over the sunset

shining stars

     in the night

     glowing over

        the world

          of light

## *Knock on My Door*

Knock on my door to ask to come in
dont want people coming in to ask me
dont like support workers tell me what to do
I want support workers to ask me not tell me
support workers to keep their promises
support workers to tell me whats happening
I need support workers to chat with me –
pointing a finger isnt nice – to listen to me
dont want support workers to talk to me
like I am stupid

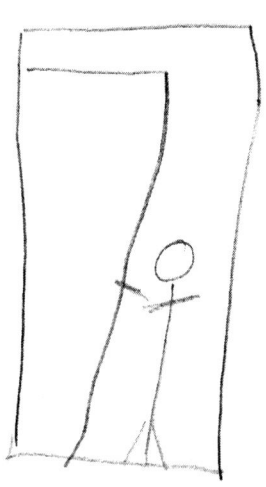

## *I Remember ...*

I had a dog called Suzy she got run over from the ice cream van and she died

When my sister Rebecca was born in hospital I came to see her with my brown coat on

I was in hospital when I was eight years old and I nearly died because I didn't get my breath back but I survived it my mum was upset and collapsed on the floor

I used to go to Jackies house to stay she looked after me when I was little

I was on a school photo with my sister

I use to go to Philippas house to stay with Gail. I use to ride on the horse with a helmet on my head and I fell off it and I cryed and Gail cuddled me

I use to pick my nose to my dad

I use to go in the Paddle Pool with my swimming costume in the front garden

I was at school with Helen and Julie

I use to go to Brownies and Guides

I am going for a Christmas dinner with the Downs Group

I went camping with school

I had an Easter egg from the Downs group

I climbed over the gate my Headmaster came for me He was angry I ran away

I use to stay at Brenda's house

I ran away from my mum

My gran and grandad took me to the eye clinic in the snow

Me and my sister were fighting on the beach and I won her

I use to sing to the camera to my Uncle David

My cousin was playing the organ

I use to live at my mum and dads house with my sister and Ruth the dog

When I first moved into my flat I was scared and nervous on my own

At Christmas time with my family I was dancing at my auntys house

I can remember Nell when she was a puppy